Email Marketing

Janet   Smith

DEDICATION

Dedicated to all online entrepreneurs

This book is a compilation of articles written on Email Marketing

Janet Smith

Article One

Aweber Email Marketing Tips

Contents

-Show Me The Money - How to Make Money With Your Email List

Introduction

There was a time where if someone wanted to do business with you they had to try to get your attention through direct mail, telemarketing or face-to-face. The problem? Most of the time these marketing methods were completely unsolicited – they were "push," as marketers pushed information to consumers. As a result, we often refer to these solicitations in a negative way and respond angrily. We use terms like:

'Junk Mail' 'Harassment' 'Snake Oil'

So how is email marketing different?

The major difference between email marketing and the other marketing methods is that people opt-in – or choose – to receive your marketing message. This is GOLDEN. It's like an open-door invitation to share your information and expertise with your customers. That, my friend, is something you just can't pay for. Convinced it's time to pay attention to email marketing? Then let's talk about where to start. In this report you're going to learn everything you need to know about starting your first email list with one of the most popular and best email software programs on the internet: Aweber.

In this report we'll cover:

Recommendation: You'll get the greatest value from this report if you follow along in real time as we discuss these topics. Even better -- you can sign up for a trial that gives you Aweber access for 30 days for only $1. Grab that and learn as you go here: http://www.Aweber.com

Just click 'order' and you'll see this:

All signed up and ready to go? Great! Let's get started.

What Is Email Marketing? We've touched a little on the concept of email marketing and how it can be a highly effective way to build your business. Now let's dig a little deeper into the concept of what email marketing is.

Let's start with some definitions:

Email List: An email list is simply a collection of email addresses. Most marketers will also collect the person's first name with the email address so that the email can be personalized through automation software. ie. Instead of just saying "Hi", you can say "Hi, Tom!" in the emails. It's also possible to collect information such as location or phone numbers so you can further segment your list and market to them based on certain criteria.

Opt-In Form/Squeeze Page: An opt-in form or squeeze page is an online form where visitors to your website or blog fill in their contact information to join your email list. With services like Aweber, that information is automatically added to your email list with no action on your part – automation is great! Subscriber: Someone who has joined your email list, typically by filling out an opt-in form. They are now part of your "list," and you can contact them via email with offers, information, updates, and more.

Email Service Provider (ESP): A company that provides the email software you can use to send out emails. In this report we're talking about Aweber, a top-ranked online ESP.

Autoresponder: A list of email messages that goes out in sequence, automatically. For autoresponders, it doesn't matter how many people sign up to your list or when they sign up. They'll get message #1 automatically, then message #2 a set time later, message #3 a set time later again, etc. It's a great way to automate parts of your business.

Broadcast: A broadcast email goes out at a specific date and time. It's different from an autoresponder as it's a one-time deal. Everyone on your list receives this broadcast message at the same time, regardless of when they joined your list. These are often used for sales notifications, special offers, time-sensitive announcements, and the like.

Like any specialty, email marketing has its own vocabulary. Knowing the basic terms will help you understand what people are talking about – including in this report!

How Do You Get Email Subscribers? Having a "list" with a fantastic series of autoresponders and broadcasts that you update regularly is great, but if there's no one on your list, you're not going to be making many sales. You need to build your list – and list-building is a specialty in and of itself.

Ultimately email marketing is a way to market your product or service through email. You can build your email list in a number of ways. Here are just a few: - Opt-In Forms. The most common way to build a list is by placing an opt-in form on a website or sales page and having people fill it out.

Whenever someone visits your blog or website, there should be a clear place for them to subscribe to receive more information from you. -Customer Lists. Many shopping carts, such as eJunkie and 1ShoppingCart, have automatic processes for adding purchasers to your email contact list.

This is something you'll definitely want to integrate, because customers are already a step above mere "prospects."

By buying something from you – even a purchase of $10 or less – they've proven that they want what you're offering, they know how to purchase on the internet and are comfortable doing so, and they have money to spend. -Forwards. At the bottom of every email you send, Aweber has an option for others to subscribe. You can add a PS or signature line that says, "Did you like this email? Forward it to a friend!" Then when that friend receives your email from someone they know and trust, they can directly subscribe to your list by clicking on the enclosed link.

Just another reason to love Aweber! -Buying Lists. It is possible to buy email lists from others. Even though this sounds like a great shortcut, I recommend against this practice, particularly when you're just starting out. Many times, lists are extremely expensive, the names and contact information are outdated, the people aren't targeted to what you're offering, and they may see contact from you as spam.

You're much better off doing things with a little elbow grease and creating your own list from scratch of people who know, like, and trust you.

Getting people on your email list may seem difficult in the beginning. There are strategies for making it more compelling for people to give you their email address, such as by providing an opt-in bonus of some sort. We'll talk more about getting targeted and interested subscribers further in this report. For now it's important that you understand you need to offer high value to potential subscribers. Now, let's talk about why building an email list might be one of the smartest investments of your time. 6

Why Build an Email List? Some people start email lists, get a few people and then give up. They get discouraged because they don't really understand the true benefits of building a large, responsive email list. Here are seven reasons why you need an email list:

Janet Smith

1. Automatically Follow-Up – An email list allows you to multiply your time in a way that would require a cloning machine! With autoresponders you can have a follow-up system in place that makes sales for you twenty-four hours a day, seven days a week.

2. Constantly Build Your Business – New prospects can be signing up to your email list automatically, every day, without your help or involvement. This is a way to be constantly building your business, automatically.

3. Capture Visitors – You've put tons of work into your website. If you're not capturing visitors, they're coming and going, possibly never to return again. If you capture their information, you can keep in contact with them and build the relationship.

4. Stay on Their Minds – Most of your potential customers or clients won't be ready to buy from you right now. Through email marketing, you can stay on their minds through your email autoresponders and broadcast messages. Then, when they are ready or in need, they'll look back for your emails or remember your website and they'll order from you.

5. Save Yourself Time – Instead of sharing your message one on one, over and over again, you can now reach one to many. This is going to not only save yourself time but also leverage your time into long-term profits.

6. Be Super-Human – It's simply not humanly possible to connect one-on-one with all your prospects and customers the way you can with an email system. The great thing is, if you set it up right your message can SEEM very customized and personal even when they ARE completely automated.

7. Increase Your Sales – Of course the goal here isn't just to be awesome (though that's a good goal in itself). What you're really looking for in an increase in sales and profits. An email list can deliver you an increase in sales.

The challenge is that if you give up too soon, you'll never see these benefits. Yes, email marketing starts out slow, but don't give up! Every marketer – even those with hundreds of thousands on their lists – started with one subscriber, then two, then ten. Yes it takes time and yes it can be frustrating waiting for the rewards but be patient and diligent, and you will see your efforts pay off over time.

Why Would You Use Aweber? Some people will start building an email list in their email account, such as Outlook. This is OK if you have only 15 or 20 people to email but when you start getting more and more prospects this can be a big problem.

For one, if you try to email hundreds of people from your own email account you'll most likely get flagged as a spammer. And secondly, by US Can-Spam laws you must have a way for people to unsubscribe from your emails at the bottom of every email.

There are plenty of email service providers out there in the cyberspace, but my choice is Aweber. Here's why:

1. High Deliverability – One of the most important factors you need to consider is whether or not your emails are getting to their targeted inboxes. If they're not, all your efforts are for nothing. Aweber provides top-deliverability to its customers. They are constantly working hard to establish relationships with internet service providers so emails from Aweber will be delivered, not diverted to the Junk Folder. Aweber has one of the highest deliverability rates in the industry.

2. Pricing – Aweber is competitive in terms of pricing. You may be able to find less expensive options, but that lower price comes at a sacrifice in terms of deliverability, options, and support. At the same time, Aweber is very affordable. You can start with a $1 trial and then continue at just $19 per month for up to 500 subscribers. With this plan you can send an unlimited number of emails per month.

3. Emails – In Aweber you have a number of features and options when it comes to sending emails. Most email software programs allow you to send both autoresponders and broadcasts but not many have a blog broadcast feature. Blog broadcasts makes are a way to send your latest blog updates directly – and automatically – to your subscribers. Aweber is also up to date in terms of social media functions, allowing you to automatically and instantly post your emails to Twitter and/or Facebook.

4. Templates – If you're not a programmer (and most of us are not!) then it's not easy to create great-looking opt-in forms or newsletters. Aweber has a very large selection of both that you can use as-is or easily customize to fit your business.

5. Customer Support –Aweber's customer support is top notch, offering phone support, live online chat, email, webinars, a free e-course, tutorials, and more.

When you start to use the program there is even a set-up walk-through. If you've got problems or questions, there are a number of different ways to get help.

6. Subscriber Statistics – Understanding how many new subscribers you have, where they come from, what they click on and when they unsubscribe is important to your business. Aweber does an excellent job of subscriber management.

One of the best features here is that you can send out
emails to your lists separately or all at once. Even if
your subscribers and on multiple lists they will only
ever get one email – a great feature to save your
subscribers the frustration of deleting multiple emails
from multiple lists. You can also view detailed reports
or even have them mailed to you.

Choosing an email service provider is an important
decision. It can literally be the backbone of your
online business so you'll want to choose wisely. The
best thing to do is write down all the features YOU
need for your business and then search for a program
that fits those needs. In most cases it will probably be
Aweber, but no matter what you choose make sure
you do it and start building your email list as soon as
possible. Then you'll be able to say what just about
every profitable email list owner says at some point...
"I wish I'd started building my list sooner!"

HTML or Text Messages or Both? When creating email lists and messages, you may wonder whether to use HTML messages, text messages or both in your autoresponders and broadcasts. Let's start with some information about the difference:

HTML – You know those emails you get that are colorful, include pictures and fancy text? Those are created with HTML code. Newsletters or 'Ezines' are often created with HTML messages.

Text – Text messages are simply, text. There is no formatting, or color, images, graphics, bolding, italics or other accents.

So... what to choose? Let's start by comparing the advantages and disadvantages of each format.

HTML emails have a lot of advantages: – Can be branded to the business look and image, conveying an overall congruity in marketing message. – Allow for easier hiding of link tracking, allowing you to see what customers click on while still making the links look user-friendly. – Formatting of text using bullets, bolding, italics, headings and other effects can increase readability of your emails.

HTML emails also have just about as many disadvantages, including: – You must create or customize HTML. This takes longer than doing plain text. – Some email providers block the HTML formatting and images, leaving you with just text anyway. – If you're looking to build personal relationships with your customers, HTML is probably not the way to go because it doesn't look like a regular personal email.

Text emails also have advantages, including: – Less likely to get filtered or blocked. – Looks the same no matter what email program it's viewed in. – Quick and easy to create and send. – Have a much more personal feel than HTML emails.

Text emails also have disadvantages, including: – No formatting, images, or branding. – Can't use hyperlinks for affiliate links or other long, ugly links. Something worth noting here is that if you do choose to use HTML then you'll also need to use text. There are a couple of reasons for this: 11

1. Some email programs will not display HTML. If you provide a text version you can get your messages through to the people using these settings. 2. Spammers use HTML messages. If you don't add a text version of your HTML page you increase your risk of getting blocked by the spam filters on a regular email account.

Ultimately what you choose is going to depend on your business needs. There is no right or wrong answer.

How to Set Up Your Email List and Opt-In Form in Aweber In this section we're going to go through setting up your email list and opt-in form in Aweber.

Step 1: Set up your email list
After you log in to your Aweber account, the first thing you'll want to do is click on the 'Create and Manage Accounts' button. It looks like this:

Then you'll need to click 'Create a New List' on the next screen:
Next, there are three sections for you to fill out: − Basic Settings − Personalize Your List − Confirmed Opt-In On the Basic Settings Page you'll find the following: List Name List Description 'From' Name Address

Notification Emails – If you want to get an email every time someone signs up to your list, enter your email address and name here. This may seem like a great idea, but you might soon be overwhelmed with opt-ins. If you choose to receive notification, I recommend setting up a separate file folder in your mailbox where these emails are automatically sent so they aren't cluttering up your in box.

On the Company Branding Page you'll find: 1. Company Branding Company Name Website URL Email Signature – This can be automatically added to all your emails.

2. Social Media/Sharing Tweet Your Broadcasts Share Broadcasts on Facebook Broadcast Archive – This allows your email broadcasts to be archived on Aweber's website so you can direct people to view past archived issues of your emails or newsletters.

3. Global Text Snippets This is another great feature of Aweber where you can set certain 'snippets'. For example, if you want to include a business phone number in your emails you may want to set it up as a snippet. That way, if your phone number ever changes you can change the snippet and not have to go back into all your emails and change it in every spot you added your phone number. Saves you time to plan ahead! On The Confirmed Opt-In Page You'll Find:

1. You Confirmation Message This is the message your subscribers will see before they confirm they signed up for your list. You can customize it for best results and a personal touch.

2. Require Opt-In on Web Forms This is the double opt-in option. It is recommended you have people confirm that they signed up for your list by getting them to double opt-in.

3. Success Page You can add a custom page for your subscribers to see after they confirm their opt-in.

Make sure you fill out each section according to the instructions and then press the save button at the bottom of each page.

Next, you need to create a web form. Click the button that says 'Web Form':

Click the 'Create a New Web Form' Button:

Now the fun starts! There are many options to choose from. Aweber has templates that would suit many different businesses. For example there are ready-made forms for people in the weight-loss, sports, pets, real estate, consulting and more.

Scan through the categories and choose your template.

Then you can use the easy editor to add text, effects, change colors and customize the form.

As usual, make sure you save the form. Click the green 'Save Web Form' button at the bottom of the screen once you're done.

Once you've saved the web form, click on the 'Settings' tab at the top of the page and fill out the basic information such as; Form Name, Thank You Page & Already Subscribed Page.

Again, click the green 'Save Web form' button. Now you're ready to add the form to your website! Click the 'Publish' tab on the page to get your code. This section allows for three options:

1. I Will Install My Form
2. My Website Designer Will Install My Web Form
3. Have Aweber Host My Form

Option 1 - This option allows you to grab coding and paste it wherever you can add HTML. Option 2 - This option allows you to simply send your web designer an email with the code to add for you. Option 3 - This is a neat option where Aweber will actually host the web form on their site. It makes for a quick way to get a web form ready to accept sign-ups. The great thing about this is you can easily build your email list, even if you don't yet have a website!

There you have it. Follow the steps in this section and you will have your first email list set up and your opt-in form ready to collect subscribers.

Before you go to much further, you'll want to add a welcome email for your subscribers by clicking on the 'Messages' tab and adding a 'Follow-Up' email.

Not sure how? No worries! Just read the next section for instructions on how to set up your autoresponders, broadcasts and blog broadcasts in Aweber.

How to Set Up an Autoresponder in Aweber

Autoresponders are email messages that are pre-set to go out at certain time intervals. For example, you could set them to go out daily, or weekly, or monthly, etc.

In the previous section I showed you how to set up your email list and opt-in form. Now once people get onto your list you'll want them to receive a nice, warm welcome message. This message will go out automatically upon signup. This is called an autoresponder.

Here's how to set up your first autoresponder message in Aweber:

1. Click on the 'Message' tab across the top of the screen. 2. Click on 'Create a New Follow Up Message'. Next, you'll want to fill out the appropriate section:

1. If sending HTML you'll need to fill out both the HTML and Text sections. 2. If sending Text then you'll need to leave the HTML section blank and fill out the text only.

Important sections to note:

Spell Check – Run your email through this quick spell check to keep it looking professional. Personalize – Use the personalization feature to call people by name, mention their location, email, etc. Attach a File – Add an attachment to your autoresponder emails. Track Clicks – You can find out what people click on within your emails. Just be aware that if you are using text-only emails then people will see the tracking links in the emails. Interval – Your first message will go out immediately, but any messages you create beyond that will need to have an interval set. The interval is the days between messages.

When you're done setting up your email click the green 'Save Message' button.

At that, you're done! You're set up with your first autoresponder message that will automatically go out when someone signs up to your email list. 20

Once you get used to this process you'll see the power having the ability to set up these automatic messages will bring. Put some time and effort into building a fabulous resource for anyone who signs up for your list and it will pay off over and over again, on auto-pilot.

How to Send Out a Broadcast in Aweber Broadcasts are email messages that go out to an entire email list, all at one time. They differ from autoresponders as an autoresponder goes in sequence and subscribers can be receiving different emails at different times depending on when they signed up. With a broadcast message all subscribers get the same message at the same time.

Broadcasts are great for time sensitive messages such as live webinars, workshops, courses, etc. They are also good for seasonal messages. Or if you just have a onetime promotion that you want to go out to your entire list.

Here's how to send one in Aweber:

1. Hover over the 'Message' tab at the top of the screen and then click 'Broadcasts'. 2. Click on the green button that says 'Create A New Broadcast Message'.

Next, you'll want to fill out the appropriate section:

3. If sending HTML you'll need to fill out both the HTML and Text sections. 4. If sending Text then you'll need to leave the HTML section blank and fill out the text only.

Important sections to note:

Spell Check – Run your email through this quick spell check to keep it looking professional.

Personalize – Use the personalization feature to call people by name, mention their location, email, etc.

Attach a File – Add an attachment to your autoresponder emails.

Track Clicks – You can find out what people click on within your emails. Just be aware that if you are using text-only emails then people will see the tracking links in the emails.

Send Immediately or Send Later – You can schedule your broadcast to go out right away or at a later date.

Send to Segment – You can segment your subscribers in many different ways. For example if you'd like to email people only signed up in the last week then choose that in the send to segment section.

Include or Exclude Lists – If you have multiple email lists in your Aweber account, you can choose to send to more than one at a time using this option.

Track Clicks – See what your subscribers are clicking on by tracking clicks. Beware these clicks are not cloaked and show up as long, messy links in your emails. You can get around this by creating hyperlinks in HTML, but there's no way around in for text emails.

Social Media/Sharing – Tweet your email or send it to Facebook with this option.

Quickstats Notification – You can find out some great stats right away by having them emailed to you.

When you're done setting up your email click the green 'Save Message' button.

Many people will use their broadcasts often but not take advantage of the abilities of autoresponders.

Here's a quick tip: Send your broadcasts out, then ask yourself if the content is 'evergreen',' meaning it never expires or becomes out of date.

If so, add that evergreen content right into your autoresponder, allowing it to do double-duty for you. That way, you'll receive the benefits of the instant message AND the long-term benefits of an autoresponder.

How to Set Up Blog Broadcasts in Aweber If you've got a blog, you're going to love this Aweber feature. The blog broadcast allows you to hook up your blog and your email list. Every time you create a new post on your blog your subscribers will get an automatic, customized email.

Here's how:

1. Hover over the 'Message' tab at the top of the screen and then click 'Broadcasts'. 2. Click on the green button that says 'Create A New Blog Broadcast'. The first thing you'll need to set up your blog broadcast is your blog's RSS Feed. Not sure what it is? Start by trying to surf to www.yourdomain.com/feed – that will normally take you to your blog feed. If that doesn't work, you'll need to check with your website designer or with the software help files.

Next, you'll need to choose a template for your blog broadcast. After you choose it you can customize the information and look   you'd like.

Important sections to note:

Spell Check – Run your email through this quick spell check to keep it looking professional.

Personalize – Use the personalization feature to call people by name, mention their location, email, etc.

Send Time – Choose what time your blog broadcast goes out.

How Often Should We Send Out Your Blog?

Broadcasts – In this section you can determine when your blog broadcast goes out. You can choose to have it go out automatically or you can have it saved in your 'Broadcasts' section so you can approve it before publishing.

Track Clicks – See what your subscribers are clicking on by tracking clicks. Beware these clicks are not cloaked and show up as long, messy links in your emails. You can get around this by creating hyperlinks in HTML, but there's no way around in for text emails.

Social Media/Sharing – Tweet your email or send it to Facebook with this option.

Quickstats Notification – You can find out some great stats right away by having them emailed to you. Using the Blog Broadcast feature is another great way to do double work. Instead of having your content show up on your blog and nowhere else, you are exposing your market to your information in more than one way. That's smart email marketing!

Finding Targeted and Interested Subscribers Now comes some real digging in and working on list-building. Don't expect your list to build itself. It's your job to get yourself out there and find as many targeted and interested subscribers as you possibly can. Here are my best suggestions:

1. Website Opt-In Form – This is an oldie but a goodie. Put a form on your website. It's not enough to put a form on your homepage saying 'Sign Up to Our Newsletter', though. You need to present your visitors with an irresistible offer, something they'll have no problem handing over their closely guarded email address for. This method can show you immediate results if you're getting enough traffic. If your traffic is low to nil, then keep reading for other great ideas to build your list. Examples are a free report, an audio or video, or a workbook. Make it valuable – this is no time to cut corners!

2. Guest Blogging – Bloggers are always looking for great, unique content. You can take advantage of this need by becoming a guest blogger. Target your blog to lead your reader to signing up to your email list. To do this you'll want the information in the blog post to be highly relevant to your email list. Deliver great information and value but leave them wanting to take the next logical step, which of course will be to sign up for your list.

3. Joint Ventures – Start making friends with other website owners. Networking with other business owners is a smart move. You'll develop relationships that can turn into win-win partnerships.

4. Advertising – Finding highly targeted websites to promote your email list on can be a great way to build a list fast. Make sure you be careful with this method as you must have a very relevant offer that visitors will respond to.

The ways to build your list are only limited by your own imagination. You will be the best person to determine how to get the most qualified subscribers onto your list.

Think about where the people you want to reach hang out. Do they visit chat forums to talk about their topic, read a certain kind of blog, visit certain news website, etc.? Your common sense and knowledge of your industry is going to lead you to the best ways. Keep trying new methods, testing the results and moving forward.

The Rules and Laws Around Collecting Email Addresses Before you start building your email list, you should know about the rules and laws that govern this industry. First off, if you are in the United States, you need to get familiar with the Can-Spam Act. Even if you are in a country that isn't governed by this law, it's a good idea to follow it anyway to be safe.

If caught abusing email and in non-compliance of the Can-Spam Act you could be subject to penalties up to $16,000.

Here is a summary of the requirements under this act:

1. Don't Use False or Misleading Header Information – The From, To and Reply To information must be accurate and not misleading in any way.

2. Do Not Use Deceptive Subjects – It is not acceptable to try to trick readers into opening emails by using deceptive email subjects.

3. Identify The Message as an Ad – You must notify your subscribers that they are reading an ad.

4. Include Valid Physical Location – You must identify your location within every email you send out.

5. Tell Subscribers How to Opt-Out of Emails – In every email there must be clear directions on how to unsubscribe from your email list.

6. You Must Honor Opt-Out Requests Promptly – You must honor opt-out requests within 10 business days.

7. Monitor Your Services – It's not ok to hire someone to help you and expect the responsibility of complying with the act transfers to them. You must be aware of what is being done on your behalf as you could be responsible for it as well.

The great thing about Aweber is that it helps you do many of these requirements automatically. For example your physical location is added automatically to the bottom of each email.

You also have directions on how to opt-out of your Aweber email lists automatically added to the bottom of each email. Finally Aweber unsubscribes people immediately upon request, so no worries about getting yourself in trouble with the 10day removal time frame.

In most cases you'll have nothing to fear, especially if you use Aweber. Just make sure you know, understand and follow the laws.

Running your email in a manner that gives your subscribers the ultimate in freedom and respect will produce a seriously high quality list. This is a list that will appreciate that you value them as people and will respond by being loyal, dedicated subscribers that actually READ your emails. Now that's a win-win situation!

Email Marketing Statistics & Reports

Congratulations! If you've followed through this report in order while taking action along the way, you've got yourself an email list with Aweber and you've added some fabulous subscribers to that list. I'm truly excited for you. You now have the opportunity to use the latest technology to connect with your market in a way that just wasn't even possible twenty years ago.

One of the most revolutionary things about your email list is its ability to give you very detailed statistics and reports. Aweber is an industry leader in analytics at just about every step of the way in your email marketing process.

Let's review some of the most useful features for your business: Email Opens & Click Tracking Want to know how many people opened your email? Want to know WHO opened your email? Better yet, want to know what they clicked on after they opened it? Maybe you'd like to know what they clicked once they got to your website? Or maybe you'd like to know if a sale resulted from that click.
This is all possible with Aweber's Email Opens & Click Tracking system.

Below is a screenshot of the detailed stats you get with every single email you send out. You can click on any tab to get more details about:

– Opens – Clicks – Sales (if you set this tracking up) –
Web Hits (again, needs to be set up) – Unsubscribes

– Domains

Below the chart it also breaks down clicks by
individual email accounts.

Email Split Testing Not sure which subject line will
work best? Want to send your subscribers to two
different salespages to see which converts
better?Then you need split testing!

Aweber handles this for you. As long as you have at
least 100 subscribers you can split test your emails.
This means your email can be divided up two to four
ways between your subscribers. What you do is select
what percentage goes out to each section.

Let's illustrate with some examples:

1. 50/50 Split Test – If you want to just send have of your list one email and half a second email then you could do a straight 50/50 Split Test. 2. 10/10/80 – If you have a large list try this trick. Send one email to 10% of your list and another to 10%. Wait and see which performs best and then send THAT one to the remaining 80% of your list.

Email Marketing Reports What if you need a larger snapshot of what's going on with a particular email list? Maybe you want to know how many subscribers you're getting daily, or how many people are opening up your autoresponders, how many people are actually verifying their subscriptions versus not, etc. All of this and more is available in the Reports section of Aweber:

Statistics can help your email marketing a lot. The gang over at Aweber really get this and that's why they've put so much effort creating user-friendly, beautifully designed and detail rich statistics.

I recommend when you get to the point of having an email list and a few good subscribers, I would recommend you take full advantage of these features. It would be a shame to let them go to waste!

Show Me The Money! How Do I Make Money From My Email List? We've talked a lot about the technical details: choosing what type of email to send, getting your lists set up, the rules and laws, etc. But what about the practical art of making money from your email lists?

I call it an art because once you develop the skill of selling to your list, you're truly an email marketing artist. When you really understand how to send out an email that gets attention and results, you've mastered an art that not everybody will be able to conquer.

Let me make sure there's no misunderstanding here: You CAN master sending profitable email messages. Quite simply it comes down to making offers that match your subscribers' interests.

When people first start an email list they are thrilled to have a medium by which they can share information to a large group of people. Most people share freely with no hesitation. When it comes to selling, however, they freeze up and shut down. They think... "My list will leave me if I send them too many promotional emails!" or "I'll get reported as a spammer!' Wait! We didn't just go through all the work of setting up your email list only to give all your knowledge and expertise away for free!

I have good news for you: The best marketers don't SELL, they simply connect people with what then need when then need it.

Let's get back to that question of how with the two main ways to sell to your email list:

1. The Information Sell – There are going to be many people who come to your email list just for information. They're just not in the mindset to buy and they're not ready to buy, yet. It's your job to show these people that they can trust you 110% percent. You do this by providing high quality information that is useful to them but also not entirely complete. This way they'll take your information and come back for more (versus taking it, getting everything they could ever wish for, and never coming back again). But here's the catch: If they want 'more' it's going to cost them. At the point where you've given away great value that leads to more value, it's really not a difficult sell.

The Information Sell can come in many forms, including:

- free ecourses - free reports - free webinars or teleseminars - free tools & templates

If that sounds overwhelming, you might want to check out EasyPLR.com to get content that's copy and paste ready for you to send.

2. The Straight Sell – There are going to be people on your email list who are ready to buy right away. They are looking for a solution to a specific problem or need and if your product fits the bill they will buy it. Don't neglect these people by not sending them direct, to the point sales offers. Tell them what you have for sale, what it does and how they can buy it. The people ready to buy it will appreciate you making it easy for them, and the people not ready with either delete or file it away for later.

If you feel unsure of where to start and what to write to your email list, think of your potential customer. What do they need?
 What problems might they be facing? How can you help?

Your best solution to 'email marketing writer's block' is to put yourself in your shoes, use your own creativity and start communicating!

Don't be afraid of messing up. Do you always say the right thing to the right people in your daily life? Of course not! You flub up. Expect you'll make a mistake or two, even EMBRACE those mistakes. Wait for them and then when they come be happy since that fear is no longer holding you back.

When it comes right down to it selling to your email list is about communication. The only way to communicate with people is to start talking. Then ask for a response.

You may not get a written response but your list responds by either unsubscribing, clicking, buying, etc. Pay attention to these actions and bit by bit you'll get on the same wavelength as those you're looking to sell to. That's when you'll turn from 'annoying salesman (woman)' to the business owner who 'gets our needs and delivers   true value'.

Article Two

Table Of Contents

Introduction

Using the electronic mailing system otherwise known as the email is one way of sending a commercial message to a target group audience. This is done for the purpose of getting the desired attention for the business through internet marketing platforms. You get all the help and info you need here.

Email Marketing Mogul Tips For Email Campaigns That Really Work

Section 1:

Email Marketing Basics for Internet Marketing

Emails can function as various different avenues to get the attention of the intended party. Some of these functions may include sending ads, requesting business participation, soliciting sales or donations and may other internet related business propositions.

The Basics

This form of communication is ideally meant to build some level of trust, loyalty and brand awareness. The email marketing exercise can be done through a cold list or form a current customer database thus the range of the target audience can be almost infinite. This internet marketing through the email platform is also meant to create other idea scenarios.

These may include the sending of email messages with the specific intention of facilitating the avenue of building a relationship between the merchant with its available customer base while at the same time tapping into the previous and possible future customer bases.

This is done primarily to foster better ties so that these emails can eventually function as a way to acquire new customers or convince existing customers to make an immediate purchase.

Some may even use the email tool to send messages to their customers regarding beneficial and supportive things available at other companies or sites for purchase which they perceive to be helpful to the customer.

There are several types of email styles that can be used for the purpose of conducting internet marketing exercises, such as email newsletters, transactional emails; direct emails and all these have their own individual advantages. Also using the emails in this fashion will be comparatively a cheaper form of advertising for the business.

Section 2: **Keep It Relevant, Short And Sweet Synopsis**
The popular saying that time is money is very true more so in today's very pressed for time world.

There does not seem to be enough time for anything and more often than not emails get deleted even before they are opened because people simply do not have the time to spare with what they perceive to be a waste of theirs.

To The Point

Therefore is one is intending to use the email campaign as an effective tool for internet marketing some very important rules or recommendations should be very carefully considered.

The primary points that often cause an email to be disregarded often lies in the actual design and presentation of the said email. In order to gain the attention of the potential viewer the email presentation has only a very small fraction of time to grab the individual's attention.

If this is not done almost immediately, then the opportunity is definitely lost and thus the email discarded.

Next if this attention grabbing point has been successfully addressed then there needs to be some thought given to the relevance of the email content. If the target audience deems the material irrelevant to them again the possibility of discarding the email is high indeed. Therefore it is important to consider if the material is not only relevant but as informative as possible without seeming too technical or boring to ensure the receiving party is happy to be included in the list of the particular email campaign exercise.

Also because time is money there should be some consideration given to ensure the content is designed to be short and to the point.
Without being too pushy in the sales pitch the product must be featured and all positive points made within the shortest possible amount of words. Including some eye catching visual effects might help too.

Section 3: **Don't Be So Formal, Write With Personality**

There are many ways to design email content to act as the first presentation material the potential customer is going to be viewing. However perhaps the most important point to keep in mind is to consider and ensure the content is designed according to the receiving party's perception of what is acceptable and impressive and what is not.

Show Yourself

There is a fine line between being too formal and being too casual, thus careful consideration should be given to the intention of the email, the product being touted and the person receiving it.

Loosely meaning that if the recipient is to be addressed in his or her capacity as a member of a company and representing its interest then the email may be expected to take on a more formal tone but if the email is meant to tweak an individual's interest on a more personal basis then perhaps the tone should be changed accordingly to a less formal one.

However having said this, it would also not really serve any purpose to keep the tone of the email so formal that it becomes almost superficial and without any personal connecting connotations.

Using the personal touch as a measurable bench mark and trying to design the mail as closely as if the individual was making a presentation in person would give the email a more exciting an approachable tone.

This will also help the recipient to connect to the general content, more so if it is designed in an interactive way. The personality of the sender should ideally be felt and the email should also create a sense of comfort and trust between the two parties.

Establishing a slightly more personal platform to work on through the initial email will adequately provide for any future exchanges.

Section 4: **Using Teasers and Your Links**

The attention grabbing window is comparatively very small for most people therefore it is important to optimize any attention directed to the email especially if it is only for a second. Using tools like teasers and links if well designed will help to optimize the chances of getting and retaining the attention of the viewer.

Getting Attention

Some points to consider when designing teasers may include the following:

☐ Choosing the best medium is necessary for the success of the email design. The press medium may be chosen for it small enticing ads which usually appears on several pages leading up to the main page. Then there are the online banners and flashes which could be provocative in nature which would entice the viewer to explore further.

☐ Design the teaser to be directed at the needs of the recipient. If the product can reflect this need than the chances of perking the recipient's interest is even better. Keep the direct personal approach foremost in the design work, toward giving the perception that the recipient is the only and important element in the equation.

☐ Teasers should also be designed to attract the recipient curiosity. Curiosity always makes an individual pose questions that creates the initial exchange of ideas phase. This exchange once established is a step in the right direction and should be capitalized upon.

☐ Another beneficial element to include is the use of links. The links should further enhance the content matter as it will assist in introducing other related sites to the recipient. These links if featured from a reputable website can increase the chances of being picked up by search engines which in turn makes the contents seem more relevant and popular. This popularity angle will further perk the interest of the recipient.

☐ Understanding the profile of the recipient will lead to better usage of appropriate links whereby the potential of the email marketing style is enhanced.

Section 5: **Using The Best Frequency For Marketing Mail**

Being bombarded with emails especially if they are of the unwanted kind can not only be a nuisance but can also be quite annoying especially if time is wasted deleting them.

This unnecessary waste of resources should not be evident in the email exercise of the individual campaign as it would eventually affect its relevance.

The Timing

Therefore it is very important to decide the appropriate frequency that should be applied to suit each individual targeted through the email campaign. Overexposure is just as detrimental to any email campaign as underexposure is because this will eventually contribute to the loss of potential sales and customer interests.

Through overexposure the intended customer will feel overwhelmed with the emails sent or they may even feel they are being spammed.

With the underexposure there is the possibility of losing out on opportunities and sales which may have otherwise been successfully made because the recipient received insufficient emails and reminders.

Generally an assessment should be made on the impact the email marketing campaign is making on the customer activity and perception.

If the frequency rate is being launched at a rather high pace then the obvious results would be for the recipient to disengage themselves from receiving the emails.

This can be done by using the aggregate open and click rates that are recorded by most email broadcasting systems. Another way to make an assessment is to look at the average number of emails received in return by the subscribers over a set period of time.

This set period could be anything from one week to one year or anything to be perceived to be a suitable time gauge for the campaign.

By gathering information and studying the data from this exercise, the sender will be able to make a more informed decision on the frequency suitable for each campaign.

Section 6: **Author Great Headlines To Keep Your E-mail Out Of The Trash**

The headline of an email is often the only window the sender has to capture and retain the attention of the target audience. The impression made based on the headline posted will be instrumental in ensuring the viewer continues to show interest in the posting. Therefore it is very important to acquire the relevant skill to ensure the best choices are made in relation to the headlines.

Capture Attention

The following are some suggestions and considerations:

☐ "The secret of ..."this is a good headline because most people like the idea of being able to crack a good secret.

Fancying themselves to be part of the privileged few is enough to draw the attention of most individuals.

☐ A quick and easy……also another attention grabber because it implies the least amount of work or effort needed to get optimum results. This definitely tunes into the average individual who looks for ways to exercise the least amounts of efforts to get things done.

☐ Now you can…………. Is attention grabbing because it creates the perception of power in the individual's hands thus making the prospect of being in total control worth exploring. Besides this it also implies the encouragement and probability of being able to adequately provide solutions to problems.

☐ Being an expert of…………people are often attracted to this type of headline as they would like to explore anything that implies it can provide the platform for fine tuning skills to be the best. Everyone wants to be an authority in their chosen area.

☐ How to..........are also equally popular attention grabbing headlines and there are always an incredible amount of tips and clues on getting things done easily and seemingly painlessly.

☐ (Number) ways to.... Is purported to be the most popular by far probably because of its more concise form of providing information and tips to the subject at hand.

Section 7: **Incorporate Some Great Free Training**

Synopsis

The idea of anything free is a potential attractive attention attracting point. This is further enhanced when it promises a certain amount of skill acquiring possibilities. In order to encourage the visitor to explore further it would be beneficial to provide some type of free training session.

Freebies

The free training can also act as an incentive that can be acquired only upon committing in some way to what is being advertised.

Therefore if the visitor was interested in the training session advertised as free, then making the commitment required would pose little or no problem at all.

The free training tool can go a long way to encouraging visitors to commit as opposed to having to pay a fee to acquire the same skill elsewhere.

Free training is also a way to address any fears or reservations the visitor may have after viewing the site which the email is attempting to introduce.

If the elements featured are of a rather foreign content or nature to the visitor, then the apprehension towards committing may cause them to be unwilling but if there was a clear indication that some training would be provided for free, this initial apprehension can be positively addressed.

Any free training provided will always be able to act as a positive incentive, because for the visitor, it would ensure that he or she is better equipped to sell or introduce the product or service to others in a professional and knowledgeable manner.

The free training incentive provided can also help to portray the company's commitment levels to the potential prospect.

The willingness to provide such assistance clearly shows the lengths the company is willing to extend in the quest to provide as much assistance as possible to potential prospects. This can be a powerful tool to use to build a future loyal relationship.

Section 8: **Be Tuned Into Your Subscribers Needs**
Synopsis
Understanding the subscriber's needs is the only way to successfully make the relevant and suitable matches to ensure resources are not wasted or misused.

The most unnecessary waste of resources is evident when information is randomly sent to anyone and everyone without any consideration or direction. There is some level of compelling truth attached to the fact that one should identify the important results of what the prospect is looking for or interested in before even considering the particular individual as a suitable prospect.

Keep Them Returning

Being in tune with what people want to achieve, the ways that they would most likely be interested to achieve something and the desired outcomes all make up the information that should be considered early on when designing the email content.

Through the quest of wanting to be tuned into the subscriber's needs focusing some attention on the market areas that seems to lack relevant comprehensive and assisting information could help to provide some idea of why there is a need and how it should be addressed.

When this is adequately identified then steps can be taken to provide the information which would then clearly show the company's ability to be in tune with its subscriber's needs.

When subscribers are assured that their needs are being considered and are of the highest priority, the sense of loyalty that is formed is quite unmatched and definitely worth cultivating. This loyalty element can and usually does play a vital role in retaining the individual as a customer.

Article 3

Contents

What Should You Test In Your Email Campaign

The Email Marketing Report Card - Do You Pass?

How to Create New Content for Your Email

Campaign

Do You Know The Best Ways to Promote Your Email

Newsletter?

Creating Email Marketing That Subscribers Read

Email Marketing Tips for Your Business

The Most Common Email Marketing Mistakes?

How Email Marketing Can Grow Your Business

Running a business today involves a number of components that never existed in the past. While business owners have a much greater reach to find their consumer, they also face a great deal more competition. The businesses that are the most successful are able to think outside the box and take advantage of tools that can help to grow their business. Email marketing campaigns are one of those tools. When used correctly this can be a powerful way to grow your business.

Email marketing starts by offering the visitor something for free. It might be an e-book, a report, a monthly newsletter, or anything else that's of value. The visitor fills out your subscription form and then begins to receive the material from your email marketing campaign.

The tricky part is in offering something that is going to get the visitor to part with their personal information including their email address and that's why your offer has to be of value. Today's online users is much more savvy than in the past.

Over time the goal is to grow your subscribers. Now you have access to all of these email addresses and you might be tempted to begin sending out all kinds of content in an effort to get a sale.

Word of warning – there are laws about spamming so make sure you familiar with these. In addition, even if you aren't actually spamming you must be careful not to annoy your subscriber, because they will simply unsubscribe.

Your subscriber signs up for a particular thing and you need to respect that. You however can always offer them various options so that they can add to their subscription or change their subscription at any time.

It's a great idea to initially create groups so that those signing up are getting exactly what interests them.

For example, you might create 10 groups that include health, fitness, consumer affairs, finances, etc. Then the subscriber can choose which categories they want to receive information from. You will also be offering what it is you have for sale that fits the subscribers category or group.

Email marketing has been one of the most successful platforms for online advertising and you too can enjoy the benefits and growth from using such a tool. The goal is to grow your business and your income and each one of these subscribers is a potential cash machine. When you market right you'll get the sale, so get busy!

Types of Emails You Need to Use

If you are running online email marketing campaigns, chances are you are already using the popular newsletter format, which usually are sent out monthly or every couple of weeks. The trouble is far too many of us stop right there and don't use any other type of email campaign, and that's a big mistake! Let's look at 4 types of email, other than newsletters, that you can use to connect with your subscribers.

#1 Informational Emails

Informational emails are not very long and generally, they do not require any action by the subscriber. They are simply there to convey a message and provide information to the recipient. Examples of informational emails include 'happy birthday' messages, course ending reminders, or webinar reminders.

#2 Educational Emails: Educational emails are very popular with recipients because they help to solve some type of problem or answer a question. You can send educational emails any time you have new content, a popular blog post, or any other educational information that matches your subscribers. This becomes even easier if you took the time to group your subscribers, because that way you can send the right content to the right people.

#3 Lead Nurturing Emails: This type of email is one of the least used or when it is used it is often used wrongly. It takes a lot of time and effort to take a lead and move them through the entire sales cycle. By using lead nurturing emails, you able to help that process occur faster and you don't need to invest a lot of time.

You can set up various nurturing campaigns with 7 or 8 nurturing emails in each and then you can simply schedule them to execute over a period of time. Both 60 and 90 days are popular depending on what your product or service is.

These should be short messages that are packed with content rich information and that try to get the lead to respond to your call to action that will lead them to your website.

#4 Promotional Emails: This type of email, if not done right, can find you with a subscriber that will unsubscribe or simply trashing your message. Too many promotional emails and you will annoy your recipient. The only time you should use this is if you have a new product or service, a special deal going on, or a special event coming up. You should not use this more than a couple of times a month.

What types of emails do you use in your email marketing campaigns? Now you have some new ideas so why not give them a try.

Making Your Email Marketing Campaign Effective Email marketing is one of the hottest ways to generate new customers. By offering something to your visitors in return for their email address, you instantly have the potential for a customer. That something might be an e-book, monthly newsletter, or anything else that has value. However, not all email marketing campaigns are created equal, and so it's important that you know how to make the most of your email marketing campaign.

#1 Give Them What They Want The number one rule for email marketing to be successful is to give them what they want. If they sign up for an email newsletter than offer them options about the type of newsletter they'll get. You can create different groups and have them check a box to join a certain group.

If you are having sale you could send the information only to those with zip coded that was close enough to come into the store and not bother the rest of your subscribers that live half a world away. Bottom line - always send relevant content and you can't go wrong.

#2 Edit Then Edit Again

One of the biggest mistakes made is to create the newsletter or other material and send it out. Once it's gone there's no bringing it back. What so many don't realize is that grammar and your style are as important in your email content as it is on your blog or your website. Before you hit the send button edit and then edit again, to make sure there are no grammar mistakes and that your message flows.
#3 Create a Publishing Calendar Nothing will have your subscribers' loose interest faster than irregularity.

If you send out a message and then don't send anything for months, they'll forget about you. They'll not bother to read your next message, worse unsubscribe, or mark it as spam. So create a publishing calendar that outlines when you'll send out your message, what your email message will be, and what your message will look like.

#4 Test Mobile devices and different email clients receive emails differently. For that reason, you should send out a test email to different devices to make sure that it appears correctly on the screen.

#5 Know and Understand Spam Rules Many people send out what would be considered spam because they simply don't know that they've broken the rules. Read the Can-Spam act and you will be able to avoid getting yourself into trouble.
You are only allowed to send out bulk emails to anyone who asks to receive that email.

If you collected email addresses through correspondence but no one asked to have anything sent then you are spamming them.

These five simple steps will make your email marketing campaign become more effective.

To Buy or Build a List for Email Marketing

When it comes to email marketing, you might think it's easier and faster to buy a list, rather than take the time to build a list, so why not just go for it. Before you are too quick to take the easy way, there are some things you should be aware of that are likely going to change your mind.

That's just the beginning of why you should really reconsider the idea of buying a list. When you use a list you buy you risk:

#1 Irrelevant Contacts If a prospect hasn't ever been to your site, has never shown an interest in your products or services has never shown an interest in the resources you offer, they quite simply you are stepping into their space and interrupting them. Typically, how you land up with their email address is that they have opted in at another website, and this was likely done with the belief that their email address would be kept in confidence. When you receive their email address, you have no idea if they are interested in anything you have to offer.

#2 Having Your Email Flagged as Spam This can be very dangerous. If the recipients don't recognize your company name then they will likely more your email to their spam folder. This sends a message to your email provider to filter out your email address and you could land up on a blacklist. Once you are on a blacklist it is very hard to get off of it.

#3 Your Message Gets Lost in the Clutter You purchased the list and you certainly are not the first person or the last that will get that list. The people on that list are probably being bombarded with emails.

You yourself may have experienced it – you sign up for one thing online and suddenly within the next few days, your email box is filled with emails from people you've never heard of. Chances are the email messages that you send out from a list you bought are going to get lost among all the other emails. The money you paid for the list will be wasted. The only one benefiting will be the person who sold you the list.

How to Build a Solid Email List: The way to build a powerful email list is through opt ins from your own website.

Each lead you get from your own website is a targeted subscriber, because they came from your own page so they are familiar with what it is you have to offer. These are the types of leads that you can convert to paying customers. It might take longer to build but it's definitely worth the wait!

How to Create Tracking URLs for Your Email Marketing

Tracking URLs are useful because they allow you to determine just how effective your email marketing campaigns actually are. You should always use a tracking URL when you are directing traffic over to your landing page.

At tracking URL is a just a normal URL with what's called a 'token' attached at the end of it. Therefore, a normal URL might look like this http://www.mywebsite.com/email where as a tracking URL would look like this http://www.mywebsite.com/email/?umm_campaign=assessment.

Your landing page is the most common place for a tracking URL to be placed. You will add the link to the page you want to track and this will automatically begin to populate data about your visitors to that page. What those results look like will depend on who is providing those results. For example, Google provides tracking links, but so does Hubspot or

Clickbank. To create a campaign simply follow the instructions provided to you.

To implement your tracking URL you simply have to copy the URL the way it is given to you. You can often opt for a shortened link, which works well in social media or a full tracking link, which is what you will use in your email campaign.

Once the link is in place and out there, it will be time for you to concentrate on the marketing action information and your analytics.

This information tells you a great deal, about what is happening with your links.

It tells you things like how many times a subscriber clicks on your link. Then it tell tells you how long they stay on your page, where they go on your site, etc. It also will tell you your bounce rate, which is how many people land on your site and then immediately leave. All of this information is very important to you.

You can create a number of different campaigns. This works well for different products or email marketing campaigns. It also is helpful when you want to test different links and see which is working best. In other words, when you want to experiment with your call to action.

Not bothering to use tracking URLs is the most common mistake newcomers make. The problem is, that by doing this it's like driving at night with your headlights off and no street lights.

Every now and then when someone passes you, you get a glimpse of where you are, but most of the time you're driving in the dark. That's exactly what will happen with your email marketing if you don't take advantage of URL tracking.

Is Your Content Working in Your Email Marketing? Your email marketing campaign's success lies a great deal, in how you present your message. If you are not checking to make sure your content is working, you could be wasting valuable time and you may even be annoying your subscribers. Let us have a look at the various components of your email content.

#1 Headlines – This is the very first thing your subscriber is going to see when they first open your email so make sure that the message is clear and concise and that it is related to your subject line. You can experiment here. Maybe you want to try using a link? Maybe you want to place a call to action? When you make changes, you are going to need to analyze to see how those changes   are working.

#2 Placement of Your Content – Depending on how long your email is you may have a great deal of flexibility here. But what you need to remember is that your most important message needs to be right at the beginning of the email. That goal is to reduce the bounce rate or the rate of exit.

#3 Call to Action – What is it you want your subscriber to do after reading your email? If your call to action is not clear, concise, and strong you will not get the click through rate you desire. You should frequently check the performance of your call to action.

#4 Content Type – What type of content are you presenting? What is your message and are you getting it across in the email. Are your subscribers learning what you want them to learn? Again, you should check this often to make sure you are getting the results you want. If not, you need to change the message.

#5 Placing Social Media Links – Try to place your social media icons both at the top and at the bottom of your email.

#6 Images – Adding images to your email is okay, but remember a large number of people are picking up their email on their mobile devices, so if your images are too large and slow to load they'll hit the back button and miss your message. If you are going to use images make sure you shrink them. You may even find that images increase your click through rate when done right.

#7 Links – Many struggle with this – just how many links should there be in your email? You'll need to experiment here. If you are getting a high click through rate then try to increase the number of links. You should always have a link in the first sentence. Creating an Effective Email Subject Line

The subject line of your email is very important and so it pays to give it the necessary attention to get it right. A poorly constructed subject line could result in your emails being flagged as

spam, not opened, or a person unsubscribing. Your email subject line should always be a call to action. A call to action is the action you want a person to take. It's more than just encouragement to open the email; it's about doing something in the email. Let's have a look at creating email subject lines with a strong call to action.

#1 Make Your Call to Action Compelling Remember you have only a few seconds to grab your reader's attention as they skim through their Inbox. Make sure you include any offer in the subject line so readers immediately see what the value of the email will be. If you create a sense of urgency with your compelling offer, you'll increase the response. You can do this by using brackets in your subject line. For example, "Learn how to Use Email Marketing [Webinar in 5 Days]."

#2 Make Sure You Don't Look Like Spam You do not want your subject line picked up by spam filters or firewall filters, so you need to be cautious when you choose your words for your subject line. Careful using words like offer, free, or act now can be flagged by the spam filters. You should also not use caps or punctuation in the subject line.

#3 Make Your Call to Action Consistent Before a person opens their email, they see the subject line and a couple of sentences in the preview. Therefore, those first two sentences need to be related to your subject line. They should add to your compelling offer and they should also be action oriented. Create a link in the first couple of sentences, which will take the reader to the website page where you want them to 'take action.'

#4 Keep Your Subject Line Short You should try to keep your email subject lines short. Remember you have only 45 characters. If you go over that your reader may not see the entire subject line. You want the most compelling part of your message right at the front of the subject line.

#5 Active Tone The subject line should speak directly to your recipient and be written in an active tone using an action verb such as sign up, download, or learn how. This is the best way to get your email noticed.

The best way to figure out if your email subject line is effective is to test.

Top Tips to Help You Boost Your Email Subscribers

Successful email marketing depends on a large customer database, so you can see why it is so important to be able to attract your email subscribers. In fact, this should be a priority for any business that uses email marketing campaigns.

Research shows that around 50 percent of consumers have signed up to receive email from as many as ten brands, while 8 percent don't receive any email from any brand. This becomes a challenge for email marketers to make it into the inbox.

Brands can use a number of tactics to encourage people to signup to email marketing campaigns; including highlighting the value of these emails through the use of testimonials or you can use a statement that is clear   and concise.

You need to make sure your signup process is simple and easy to follow.

Offer Free Content One of the most popular tactics for B2B companies is to offer those that signup something free, such as a white paper, or other forms of free content that can really offer value to the subscriber. It's a great way to get people to part with their email address.

Remember the Importance of Placement If nothing else, you need to keep in mind that placement is key. You need to make sure that visitors land on your home page otherwise called your landing page, and they must immediately make the decision to signup for the email marketing campaign. Provide the option in numerous places on your site. You can place a signup box in a fixed place on your site. The header or footer work well.

Turn the Newsletter Into a Product This tactic is used by many of the multimillion dollar companies who recognize how the newsletter can be used as a powerful tool to engage your customers or potential customers. You need to make sure that your newsletter doesn't come across as spammy or you will quickly lose subscribers.

Creating a newsletter that is packed with useful information and laid out in a way that is easy for subscribers to read and understand will have more and more consumers heading towards signing up for quality emails because of the value they offer.

Your email subscribers are at the heart of your email marketing campaign and you need to recognize the numerous ways that you can increase your subscriber base and ultimately increase your revenue.

How to Get Your Email Marketing Read

It's one thing to put together your email marketing campaign, but it's quite another to get it read. Let's look at some things you can do to improve the readability of your email marketing campaign and keep people engaged.

Horizontal Viewports Your email message needs to be designed to have a horizontal viewport. Most designers know this, but what's not as well known is how small most viewports are. The normal size of the preview pane is approx. 638x86 pixels, according to recently released information by MicroMass Communications. What this means is that the first 100 pixels of your email won't be seen in the majority of cases. With the shift moving towards mobile devices, that viewing area is getting smaller not larger. So make sure you make the most of this very small space. It is the only place you get the opportunity to convince your reader to read your entire message.

Janet Smith

Email Clients Are Unforgiving Web browsers are
pretty forgiving of messy HTML or flawed code.
However, email clients are not at all this way. CSS
will be frowned on. Images that are undefined will be
tossed somewhere, and messy HTML will be rejected
not corrected. You must define the height and
width of all the images you embed. You must use
Title and Alt tags, and you must make your links
absolute. Don't do fancy unless you are sure it will
work.

The Writing Rules of the Game Use few images and
many words. Yes images are certainly eye catching
but they slow down the load time, and this is
important to many users especially those that don't
have hi-speed internet or who are using mobile
devices. Rely on text to its job. Super copy will load
fast, fits into tiny spaces, and gets your message
across.

Avoid the Use of CSS Whenever Possible Email clients and CSS don't get along all that well, so it is best to avoid if you can. Even with major email, clients there are compatibility issues, which doesn't make a lot of sense in this day and age but it will eventually improve. However, there are times when CSS is necessary for your email design. If that's the case, then you need to make sure that all of the properties remain inline and are not in shorthand. Keeping these tips in mind when designing your email will improve the likelihood that your email will be read and that makes your email marketing campaign effective.

Optimize the Delivery of Your Email Marketing
One of the most successful ways to make your email marketing successful is to optimize your delivery. One of the first things you should do is to create different groups. That way each group will receive the information that is relevant to them.

For example, let's say you sell downloadable music, tablets, and laptops. The customer that is interested in downloadable music might not be interested in laptops. By creating groups, you can clearly target your market.

Your goal isn't to be too aggressive with your selling. What you want to do is allow them the opportunity to both share and digest what it is you have to share. Create four segments and label them:

* Leads * Customers * Win-backs * Newsletters

Set Expectations Next, you need to set your expectations so you don't land up annoying those on your email list. The expectations include: * Why a person should subscribe to your list * How many emails are you going to send out * When will they receive these emails * What are the emails about * Who is the person or brand that these emails are being sent from? Recommend your subscribers add your email address to their safe list.

When done correctly you reduce the likelihood that someone will be surprised when your email arrives and then unsubscribe from your mailing list. Respecting Privacy You must always respect the privacy of your subscribers so that they remain an active subscriber. Be sure to state that you are never going to sell their information a third party. You could even create a full privacy policy so that they knew exactly how you handle their personal information. To comply with Can-Spam laws you must remove anyone that requests to be taken off the list within 10 days of that request.

By taking the time to optimize the way you deliver your email message to your subscribers you increase the likelihood of that subscriber remaining as such, and as a result, you increase your opportunity to turn that subscriber into a paying customer, at some point along the way.

Email marketing is one of the most underutilized marketing tools that are available to business owners. When done correctly it offers a high conversion rate from subscriber to paying customer, so it is definitely worth your time to learn how to carry out email marketing the correct way.

4 Tools to Optimize Your Mobile Email Marketing Campaign

Email marketing gets a lot of attention but what doesn't get a lot of attention is the mobile email marketing campaigns and yet almost 50 percent of all email marketing emails goes to mobile devices.

This is a very important trend with no end in site – when you send your next email marketing campaign out, the majority of your customers are going to read it on their smartphones not on their web browser.

This leads us to the question ' are your emails properly optimized for opens and reads, along with click through from mobile devices. Mobile open rates are around a whopping 300 percent. So, now is the time for you to start taking your mobile optimization seriously. Let's start by looking at four tools you can use to optimize your mobile email marketing.

#1 JPEG Mini We will begin with a winning app that's easy to use. Download speeds are often very slow on mobile devices, which is why it so important for you to make sure you keep the file size down. JPEG Mini is one program that can be used to significantly reduce your image size before you add them to your email. It's just a few simple clicks to reduce the size by as much as 80 percent.

#2 Litmus If you are like most you have a handful of email templates that you like to use over and over. Litmus is a tool that you can use every now and then to audit the templates you use. It will show you how your template is going to look in various email clients. It's an excellent tool to use before you launch any big campaign if your budget allows for it.

#3 Theme Forest Testing will reveal how well your templates work on mobile devices. It's common for them to be too wide or for the font to be too tiny. This will annoy your subscribers and it could have a very negative impact on your email marketing campaign. Instead, use email templates designed for mobiles devices to avoid these issues. Theme Forest is one of those programs that can help you. These templates can be customized so you get exactly what you want.

#4 Mailchimp You can easily manage your entire email marketing campaign using Mailchimp.

Mailchimp even provides a video that shows you how to create responsible emails.

To make the most of your mobile email marketing campaigns take advantage of these tools.

Successful Email Marketing

Email marketing is a powerful tool when used right converting subscribers to paying customers over time. It allows you an opportunity to easily share what you have to offer in a manner in which the subscriber is receptive, but only when it is done correctly. Let's have a look at the 9 steps you should use to enjoy email marketing success.

Step #1 Determine What Your Goal Is For your email campaign to be a success you need to know what your actual goal is. This allows you to accurately target and measure the success of your goals along the way. Here is an example of goals to consider:

* Are you successful at alerting customers of new features and products you have to offer. * DO you announce upcoming events in a timely manner and do people register for it * DO you send email to get subscribers to also subscribe to your blog and do you measure your conversion rate.

Step #2 Who Your Emails From The name and email address that you send your email from needs to remain consistent on every single email you send. That creates brand recognition and you are less likely to land in spam.

Step #3 Subject Line Your email subject line need to be a call to action for your subscriber. They need to immediately know what action is required of them and why. Remember you only have 45 characters that are visible so make sure that you use them wisely and your message does not get cut off.

Step #4 The Email Body Did you know that most people will read an email in under 10 seconds? Therefore, it is important that you are presenting the most important part of your message at the top of the email. This is also helpful because it shows as the snippet in the subscribers email program.

Step #5 Email Signature Your email signature should match the 'from' in the email. You should sign the email and include any other information you think the recipient should have such as your phone number, or perhaps your degree is important, or your web address.

Step #6 Testing Your Email

It is important that you always test your email on a number of email platforms and on mobile devices, which make up a larger percentage of where email is read. That way you can make sure that your email is coming through correctly on all platforms.

Step #7 Send the Email Always include the option to view as HTML or text. This is it! It's time to send out your email campaign and start to enjoy the benefits. Step #8 Measure In order to know if your email campaign is successful you need to measure the click through rate and the unsubscribe rate. This will help you determine what you need to change or what's working.

How to Optimize your Mobile Email Marketing

You may have created your email marketing campaign for both PCs and mobile devices. Perhaps your email marketing campaign already looks great on a mobile but what happens when the subscriber clicks on a link in your email? Where does your subscriber land up? If your mobile site doesn't have a landing page SparkPage is an app that allows you to create mobile landing pages. Of course, there are others. You can build each page in just minutes using it to provide details on a special offer.

Take advantage of Google Analytics for mobiles, which allows you track your mobile users when they visit your landing page(s). It will allow you to find pitfalls, bottlenecks, and improve your conversion rates.

You are going to want access to some good email templates. Make sure you test the templates you are going to use as many emails don't display properly on mobile devices. For example, some templates provide text that's too small or templates that are too wide. This will destroy your engagement with your subscribers. Your best bet is to seek out templates that are designed for mobiles and then you won't have to worry about problems.

Mobile CTA tracking is what you need now that your campaigns for mobile devices are completed. You can track mobile campaign goals.

You want to promote your new app to your users. You can create a unique URL for your email campaign and track the mobile installs that are generated using an app like Yoz.io. You will also want to promote your new app to your users and the best way to do that is by emailing to their smart phone. You can use something like LogMyCalls to track the number of calls being generated by your email marketing.

The main thing to remember and focus on when working on optimizing your email marketing campaign for mobile devices is to use tools that are designed for mobile devices. That will eliminate a lot of the hassles you can run into.

Mobile email marketing is a very important tool for today's consumer. Email marketing should no longer just focus on email clients for computers.

If you want to maximize the value of your email marketing campaign your focus should include mobile devices. In fact, a great deal of focus should be put on the mobile side of your email marketing and you will maximize your sales.

What Should You Test In Your Email Campaign
Did you know there are elements of your emails you can test in your email campaigns? Testing your emails is very important to decreasing the number of people that unsubscribe and increasing your click thorugh rate. Your goal is to determine what components of your email need to change if you want to get better results.

#1 The 'From' Name and Address You can easily test who and where your emails are coming from. It is important to keep the name and address consistent on all of your emails. Test by sending a few emails to yourself to make sure you have impact you want.

#2 Subject Line This is a very important part of your email. You should test the following to ensure they are the way you want them and they are working the way you want them:

* Adding a personalized message to the subject line * The length of the subject line * The call to action * The words you use in the subject line

#3 Email Design It's a god idea to have one main template that you use all the time. Having slight variations is okay, but you don't want huge differences because you are looking to build familiarity and at the same time impact. You will want to evaluate your design periodically to make sure it is still working and if not, then you will need to make changes. Design elements you can test include:

* Capitalization * Bolding * Font size * Images * Font Colors * HTM vs. plain text

#4 Email Content It's a good idea to test the content of your email. After all, you need to make sure that you are creating the response you are looking for. You can test the following: * Headlines – Since this is the first thing, anyone sees it should always be consistent with your subject line. You can experiment here. Maybe make it a link? Bold it? Etc. but you need to test what works. * Placement of your content – Experiment with moving your content around to different areas in your email.

Just remember the most important content should be at the beginning. * Call to Action – This is very important! This is what creates the environment for your subscriber to take further action, so you need to test to make sure you are getting the desired click through rate. * Placement of Links and Images – Both are okay in your email but don't go overboard, and make sure your images are small enough that they will load quickly.

Timing

Finally, check your timing. Test to see if the email are going out at a time that's effective. You can date time stamp your emails so you know when they are picking them up after you sent them.

What you want to test in your email marketing campaign might vary from one person to the next, but what's important is that you do this and you do it on a regular bases to make sure you are getting what you want from your emails.

The Email Marketing Report Card - Do You Pass?

Anyone can through together and email and send it out to subscribers. Even building subscribers isn't terribly difficult. Most people will sign up if you are offering them something of value that they want. But creating an email marketing campaign that's highly effective and creates a high click through rate is not something everyone does well. As a result, many many people are wasting their time sending out emails and not getting   the results they want.

Let's have a look at this email marketing report card and you can decide if you pass or fail. You can also decide where you need to make changes to increase your click through rate.

#1 Does your email have a goal? What is the purpose of your email? Are you telling your subscriber what you want to share and what you want from them? Email should always be action orientated. And your message should be clear and concise. Test it. Ask someone not familiar with what you are doing to read your email and get their response.

#2 Do you have a real person, company, or brand in the 'from' name box? You need to make sure that your email is coming from someone real. These day's people are much more cautious and if they cannot connect the email to someone real, it's going to land in the trash or even in their spam.

#3 Does your email address come from a real person? You should not be using email addresses like admin@ or sales@ These will not be nearly as effective as using an email address that's from a person like sally@ or john@. Subscribers want to connect with real people.

#4 Does your subject line contain an action oriented or compelling subject? Your subject line should contain a call to action. However, you only have 45 characters here so use them wisely. A common mistake is to have a subject line that is too long. It then gets cut off and ruins your message. Go for short and sweet – keep it easy to understand. In this case, less is better.

#5 Do you have at least two links in your email? Have you made use of an anchor text link in the first sentence? You need to! You can place links with tracking URLs in the rest of the email.

#6 Does your email comply with CAN-SPAM Law? This is very important; otherwise, you're going to find your email in the spam folders. To comply you must include your company name and address as well as an unsubscribe link. If someone wants to unsubscribe you must do this within 10 days of being notified.

That's it – well did you pass? If yes – congratulation! If no – that's okay, because now you can get to work fixing.

How to Create New Content for Your Email Campaign

Whether you have ran an email campaign for some time and are running out of ideas or you are new to email campaigns and aren't sure what type of content to use, you'll find these ideas offer a great way to expand your reach, keep your current subscribers, along with obtaining new subscribers.

Your goal is to generate leads from your site by offering visitors relevant content. You must always have in your mind the question "What's in it for me?" That's what visitors are always asking themselves before signing up for what you have to offer. Your job is to make sure you are offering something that answers that question in a manner that will have your visitor subscribing.

Types of content you can offer are numerous. Let's have a look at a few great ways to hook your visitor.

1. E-book or whitepaper – Create around six blog posts that discuss a similar topic(s) and then combine them to make yourself an e-book or whitepaper. Depending on the length of the blog, you might need more post. Feel it out as you go.

2. How to Guides – People want to know how to accomplish all kinds of things. All you need to do is create a simple guide for your visitors that they can download. For example, perhaps you sell an analytics product, and then create a guide on how to effectively use this kind of product.

3. Top Industry Trends – This could be the top 5, top 10, etc. whatever you have to work with. Write a quick introduction on these new developments in your industry and write about these developments telling the reader what you think about each of them.

4. Create a video of the product – Videos have become very popular and at no time has it been easier for anyone to upload a video and then share it with the customer and prospects. Create a video showing all the features of your product, how to accomplish a specific goal, or whatever else. Then use that video to have them move forward in the sales funnel.

5. Checklist – You can create a checklist that is made up of steps that your visitor can use to solve a specific problem. For example, if your visitor is looking to use Facebook pages, you could create a checklist that walks them through the process.

You now have five types of content you can use to engage your visitors and have them commit to being a subscriber. Why not give them a try?

Do You Know The Best Ways to Promote Your Email Newsletter?

If you've are just in the process of starting a newsletter, congratulations! Perhaps you are getting a few new subscribers each week but for the time it's taking you to create your newsletter you really want to see subscription at least over a hundred and eventually much higher. How do you do this? You promote your email newsletter the same way you would promote your website or your blog.

You need to create: * A call to action – Should express the frequency and the theme of the newsletter. Should say something like "Sign up for our Weekly Newsletter Featuring Email Marketing.

* A landing page – Describe why a visitor should subscribe, the frequency of your newsletter, the content, testimonials from those already receiving the newsletter, even a screen shot of the newsletter.

* The form page – This should be short and include first name, last name, social media info, company, email address. The briefer the form the better. You might not even include the last name.

* A thank you page – This page should once again tell the subscriber when they would receive the newsletter, and how they should add the sending email address.

Promoting Your Newsletter

Promoting your newsletter can be a lot of fun. Let's look at ways you can accomplish this.

#1 Blog Be sure to have a call to action in the sidebar of your blog and at the end of some of the blog posts. A call to action with your email newsletter is at the top of the funnel call to action, which generally performs the best in blog content.

#2 Website Call to Action You should have at least one call to action on every website page. In fact, it's a lot better if you have can have two to three calls to action on each page.

#3 Emails that Nurture Leads To promote your newsletter set up a lead nurturing email. It's an excellent strategy because it will show how interesting s. Each time they receive your newsletter they will grow a little and possibly decide they would like to do business with you.

#4 Landing Page Form On your landing page, add a field form asking if they would like to subscribe to the newsletter. It's an easy way to grow your subscribers.

You should promote your newsletter every chance you get. Have your visitor fill out the form to subscribe and get on the list to receive the newsletter. Creating Email Marketing That Subscribers Read It seems like just yesterday that emails had been straight text with no formatting and no images. But over time this changed and design became part of emails. Color and layout then become popular almost to the point of gaudy and now it seems we've pulled it back a bit again. No more big ugly links, no more animated graphics and no more color palettes that leave you running screaming from your desk. So what's the right way to do an email marketing campaign? How do you ensure your subscribers actually read what you send out?

Stay Within the Ability of the Email Client: The most important thing you need to remember is that while you can create incredibly fancy emails the purpose of email is to deliver a fast and efficient message. Browsers have evolved, but email clients mostly refuse to make change and so what looks good on a web page may look terrible in email or it may not even load properly.

Just the Basics Keep your design simple, which will keep your life simpler, and your subscribers happier. The more intricate your layout design the more opportunity that something will go wrong. Think old school and most of all make sure you test enough. What will work right with one email client may not work right with another email client. The only way to know is to test properly.

Place a Link at the Top Sometimes email messages come through as garble if the transmission is interrupted or other glitches occur. This is why you should have a link to a web page that's the same as the email message, and that link should be right at the top. Don't use this link for anything else or you could annoy your subscribers.

The Landing Page You might already be familiar with the importance of your landing page. It should be very interesting and it should hook, grab, and pull your viewer in quickly.

You only have seconds before your visitor moves on. Make sure your landing page is working properly and that links go to pages that are working. Once again, testing and ensure there are no problems.

Stay on Topic The subject line is an important component of your email marketing campaign. This is the most immediate connection between you and your subscriber and it lets them know what to expect in the email. That means it needs to grab their attention. Make your subject line: * Personnel * Ask a question * Use a punch line * Use a number (5 solid tips)

And remember to keep your subject line brief. Creating an email marketing campaign that's successful isn't as difficult as you might think.

Email Marketing Tips for Your Business

Email marketing is an excellent way to connect with your customers without having to spend a whole lot of money. Newsletters are one great way to get people to sign up. Here are 5 email marketing tips your business should implement.

1. Make subscribing easy – Create a form for sign up on your home page, Facebook page, blog, and wherever else potential customers are already found. Collect names and email addresses. You could collect birthdays to provide a free gift, invite visitors to join groups, etc. Just don't include too many fields because if it takes too long to subscribe you'll scare visitors off.

2. Let your subscribers know what they can expect from you – What will you be sending? Newsletters, daily deals, weekly tips, company updates, etc. Give them all the information you can on your sign up sheet, and even let them choose what they'd like to receive.

3. Send out an email to welcome your subscribers – Sending out a welcome email makes the client feel good, and it reminds them why they are on the list. You can let them know that there's

good things to come and even give new subscribers a special offer.

4. Make sure your newsletter fits your brand – When creating your email campaign you need to make sure that you match the look and feel of your brand. If you are taking advantage of a template to create your newsletter, then you need to customize it with your company colors and include your logo. Creating consistency creates familiarity.

5. Send subscribers the type of content that you want – For example, if you are offering a newsletter then make sure that the content that is in the newsletter is relevant to your market. If you have different email campaigns for different groups then you need to make sure that each group is getting content that is relevant to them. There's no faster way to lose subscribers than by not offering them something they are interested in. In addition, it needs to remain fresh and current.

Email marketing remains one of the leading ways to grow your customer base. You first bring visitors on board because you offer them something they are interested in and then you can sell them something. What makes email marketing so powerful is that you can continue to sell them different items that are relevant over and over. Building your customer database through email marketing is building yourself an repeating income.

The Most Common Email Marketing Mistakes?

Email marketing can be a very effective sales tool; however, it sometimes gets a bad reputation, because those using it don't understand the correct way to make use of it. Like any marketing tool, it can be used correctly for great success, or poorly and destined for failure. There are some common email marketing mistakes that are often made. These can really destroy any benefit from using the email marketing strategy.

Mistake #1 - Taking up too much of the Recipients Time One of the most common mistakes made by those implementing an email marketing campaign is to not think about your recipient's time. There's a good and bad time to send emails. And realistically there are a lot more bad times than good. There are many webinars and helpful tools online to help you determine when would be the right time for the kind of message you are going to send. It matters because if the message shows up at the wrong time it is much more likely to simply be deleted without ever being opened.

Mistake #2 - Not Using an Email Service Provider (ESP) If you want to effectively send emails to your lead, you need to take advantage of an Email Service Provider. Why? Because they will ensure that all of your emails are clean, CAN-SPAM compliant and ready to be sent out.

Now a days there are just so many ways that your email message can be marked as spam. It might look fine to you but still are picked up as spam, which is why you need to be using an Email Service Provider so that you can ensure you get the assurance that your emails are actually reaching their destination and that your subscribers are reading them.

Mistake #3 – Image Overload Images can really add to your content when done correctly, but the trouble is they are seldom used correctly. Two common mistakes include using too many images and using images that are too big. Remember that a large number of your recipients are going to receiving their email on their mobile devices and if the images are too big they'll be very slow to load and you will frustrate your recipient. Too many images can lead to loss of your message. So what you want to do is use one or two images that have been shrunk in size and that help grab the reader's attention to your message.

Avoid these three common mistakes and you will be on your way to a successful email marketing campaign.

Have you bought this book?